APES and MONKEYS

by
John Grassy

Scientific Consultant:
Colleen M. McCann, PhD
Wildlife Conservation Society

Copyright © 2007, 1999 Kidsbooks LLC
www.kidsbooks.com

Manufactured in China

0507-1C

Visit us at **www.kidsbooks.com**®

CONTENTS

◄ Great acrobats, these two orangutans hang tight for a kiss.

HUMANLIKE?

How closely related are apes and monkeys to people? They, like us, belong to a group of mammals known as "primates." Primates share certain traits. We have thumbs that can grasp things, eyes positioned at the front of our head, and a large brain. Also, apes and monkeys, like people, have a social life.

A WILD BUNCH

Apes and monkeys do wild things, like beating their chest, swinging from trees, and howling day and night. These highly advanced creatures also do much more. They show feelings of affection. They fight and make up. Some have even learned to use tools.

6

▼ MONKEY SEE...

Talk about smart! Apes and monkeys are very fast learners. A young female macaque discovered that dunking a sweet potato in the sea was the easiest way to clean sand off. In a short time, her family and friends, then the entire group, started washing their potatoes.

WHAT'S A LEMUR? ▲

The lemur is a prosimian—a relative of apes and monkeys. Found only on the island of Madagascar, the ring-tailed lemur looks more like a cat than a monkey—with its whiskers and large ears.

THE SPECIAL ONE

The tarsier is in a group by itself. To *primatologists,* the people who study primates, this creature has a strange mix of traits. It has the large eyes and ears of the prosimians. But it also has a short, furry nose like monkeys and apes.

WHAT A LIFE!

Compared to many animals, monkeys and apes live a long time. In the wild, monkeys can live for 20 years or more, and gorillas, chimpanzees, and orangutans may live past the age of 40.

7

MANY MONKEYS

The world has a lot of monkeys, about 130 species. Those that live in South and Central America are called New World monkeys, and those found in Africa and Southeast Asia are called Old World monkeys.

A langur from Asia ▶

BIG AND BAD ▼

Baboons are the largest monkeys—and they're tough characters. This comes in handy around the lions and hyenas in Africa. Baboons spend the day on the ground, but sleep in trees or cliffs at night for safety.

LITTLE CRITTER ▼

The smallest New World monkey is the pygmy marmoset, just five inches long with an eight-inch tail. It lives in the rain forests of several South American countries. Like other New World monkeys, it spends most of its time in trees.

COLORFUL DIANA

The Diana monkey is a member of the guenon family, the most common group of monkeys in Africa. Guenons have long arms, legs, and tails, and brightly colored coats.

8

ABSOLUTE APES

The ape family has just four members: gibbons, chimpanzees, orangutans and gorillas; the last three are known as the "great apes" due to their size and body shape. They live only in Africa and parts of Southeast Asia.

▲ High above the forest floor, 20 to 100 feet, orangutans spend much of their day swinging from limb to limb looking for food.

APE OR ▲ MONKEY?

Besides their large size, apes are different from monkeys in other ways. They don't have a tail, and they "knuckle-walk" on their front hands. Monkeys scamper about on the flats of their palms, much like a squirrel.

ACROBAT

Smallest of the apes, the gibbon has very long arms for its size, and uses them to swing through the trees. It can also walk along a branch using only its two legs, holding both arms out for balance.

SUPER SILVERBACK

Apes are big—really big. The largest and most powerful of all is the gorilla. A mature male "silverback" stands more than 5 1/2 feet tall and weighs an average of 350 pounds. Gorillas lead a quiet life, eating massive amounts of leaves, stems, bark, and roots.

LIVING ROOM

Apes and monkeys live in tropical forests and grasslands. They eat fruit, nuts, grass, leaves, insects, and other small animals.

The white-faced saki lives in South America's Amazon basin.

REAL SURVIVOR

In South Africa, the chacma baboon lives in deserts and plains, as well as along the rocky seashore, where it feeds on crustaceans. At night it sleeps on boulders or rocky cliffs.

▼ STAY AWAY!

Each group of apes and monkeys needs a place to call its own. White-handed gibbon families live in the forests of Southeast Asia, and they don't like trespassers. Each morning the male and female sing a duet for as long as 15 minutes, sending a message to other gibbons to stay away!

OUT ON A LIMB ▼

In the dense canopy of Brazil's rain forest, the golden lion tamarin eats, sleeps, and travels. To avoid predators, most forest-dwelling monkeys, such as tamarins and marmosets, sleep in the hollows of trees—a tough spot for a jaguar to reach.

SNOW MONKEY

The Japanese macaque has adapted to a harsh environment. On rugged Honshu Island, these monkeys endure snowy winters in the mountains. Once the trees have shed their leaves, the macaque gets through the cold season by feeding on bark.

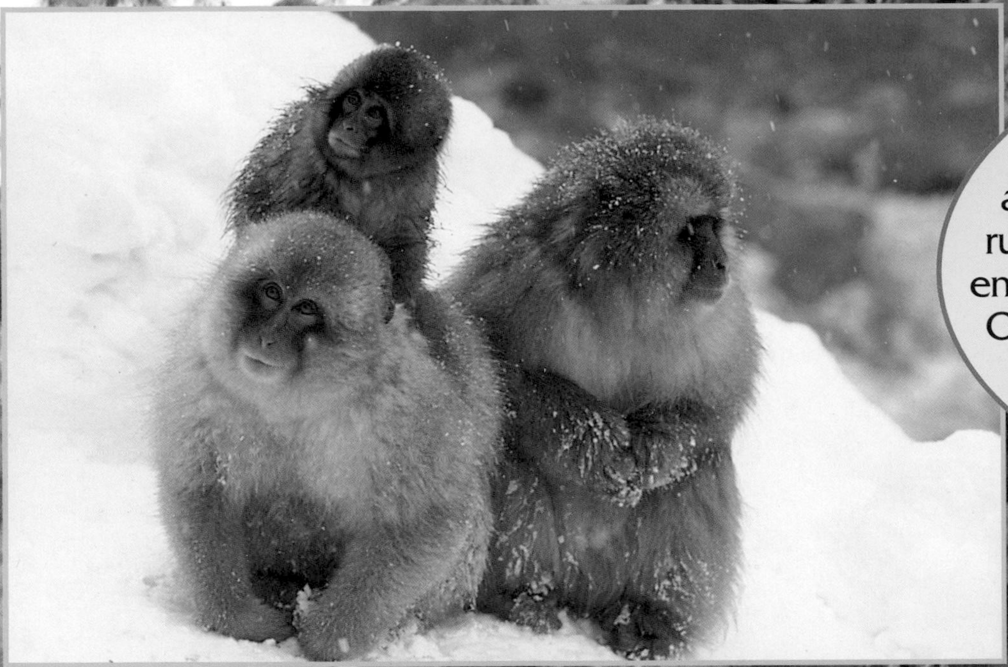

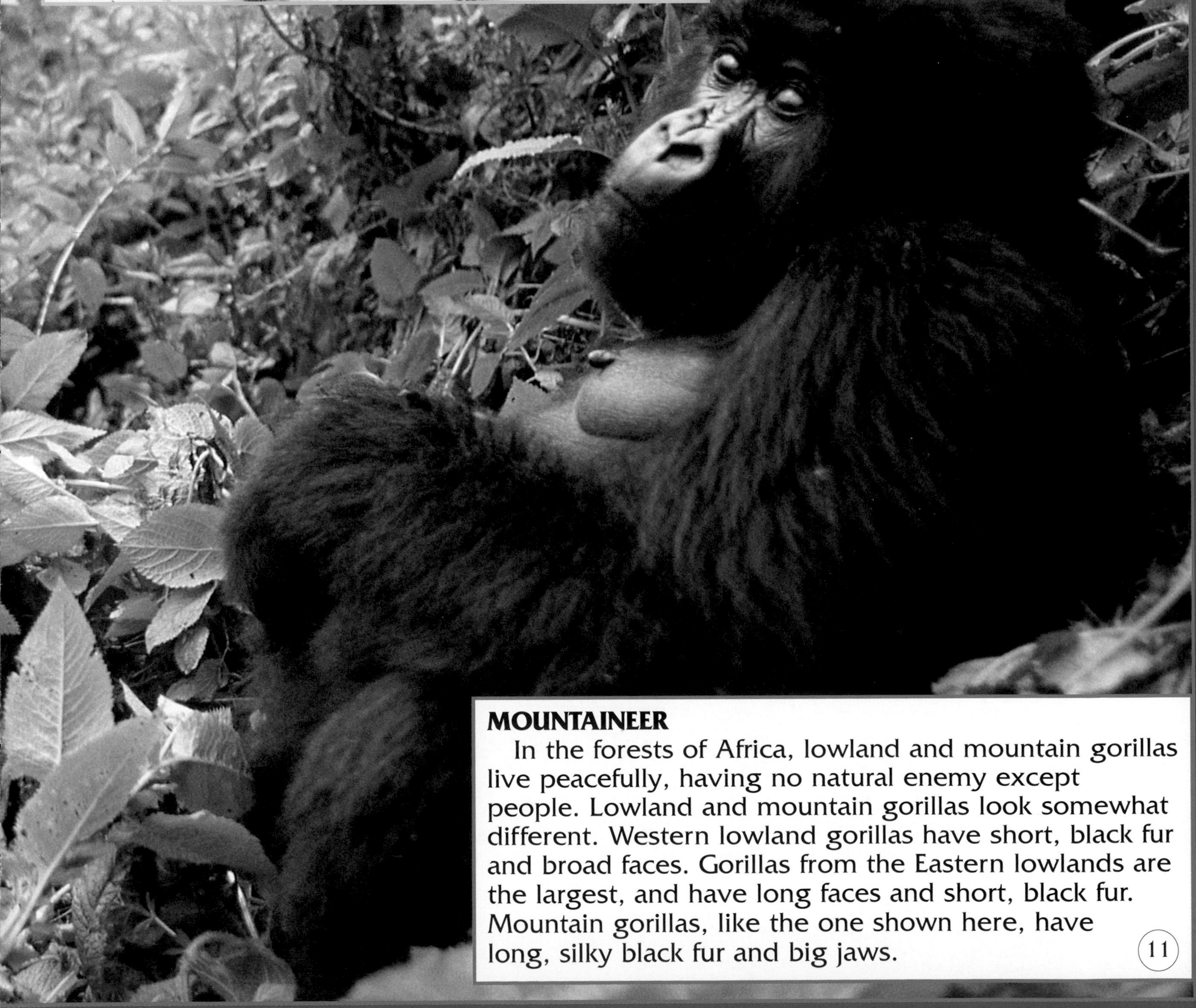

MOUNTAINEER

In the forests of Africa, lowland and mountain gorillas live peacefully, having no natural enemy except people. Lowland and mountain gorillas look somewhat different. Western lowland gorillas have short, black fur and broad faces. Gorillas from the Eastern lowlands are the largest, and have long faces and short, black fur. Mountain gorillas, like the one shown here, have long, silky black fur and big jaws.

AMAZING BODY

Apes and monkeys are built for a life of climbing, grasping branches, and collecting food.

TALENTED TAIL

Like many other monkeys, the spider monkey can grasp a tree limb with its tail and hang safely while collecting fruit with both its hands.

SEEING STRAIGHT

Like people, apes and monkeys have *stereoscopic* vision, which enables them to judge distances. That's very important if you're an acrobat like the black-and-white colobus monkey, leaping high above the ground from one branch to another.

HANDY THUMB

Try to pick up a pencil using only your fingers, not your thumb. It's difficult. Using your opposable thumb makes it easier, because it can press against the fingers like a clamp. Apes and monkeys have a thumb, too, which helps them groom, pick leaves, and clamber up trees.

WISE GUY

Apes and monkeys are known for their intelligence. Next to people, gorillas and chimpanzees are thought to be the smartest of all animals. Chimps have even learned to strip twigs of leaves and use them to fish a termite dinner out of a nest.

ON THE MOVE

Monkeys can really move through the trees, but the ape known as the gibbon is the champion swinger. It makes spectacular leaps from one tree to another, or it *brachiates* (BRAY-kee-ates) from limb to limb—using its long, powerful arms. It grabs a branch and swoops downward, then reaches with the other hand for another limb and keeps on swinging!

PADDED SEAT

Old World monkeys, such as baboons, sleep sitting up, and they have a built-in cushion for comfort. Look on each side of the tail and you can see their two hairless pads of skin, called *ischial callosites.*

The hair of apes and monkeys offers protection from rain, wind, and biting insects. It often needs cleaning, and fellow troop members are eager to groom a friend.

IN THE CHEEK

Some monkeys have a special place for storing food—in cheek pouches! Baboons, macaques, and other monkeys stuff food into the pouches and snack on it later!

TALK ABOUT IT

Great communicators, apes and monkeys have many ways of warning each other of danger. And they have many ways of letting family or group members know what's on their mind.

Howler monkeys are known for their howl, which sounds a little like a dog's bark and can be heard up to two miles away.

LIP ACTION

Lip-smacking is used by monkeys as a friendly invitation for another monkey to approach. Goeldi's monkey opens and closes its mouth rapidly, and sometimes even sticks its tongue out!

CHIMP PALS

Friendships between chimpanzees are very strong and can last for years and years, even if one chimp should take up with another group. When two chimp friends meet after a period of separation, they throw their arms around each other, hug and kiss, and pat each other on the back.

ENEMY ALERT

The vervet monkey of Africa has developed specific alarm calls for each of the major predators it faces: eagles, leopards, and snakes. Group members will look up at the sky, run up a tree, or quickly climb even higher into the trees, depending on which predator is at hand.

PASS IT ON

When apes and monkeys think of a solution to a problem, the word gets around. One group of chimps that learned to use twigs to fish for carpenter ants passed on this technology to another community living some distance away.

TOUGH GUY

Baboons are tough characters, and the leader of the troop is the toughest of all. Feared and respected by his fellow baboons, the leader may only need to glare at an upstart male or a youngster causing too much mischief—and the problem is solved.

FANGS

Watch out for those teeth! Apes and monkeys have pretty sharp canines, which are sometimes used to threaten other troop members, or to defend against outsiders.

GETTING TOGETHER

Most apes and monkeys live in groups, or troops, in which they grow up and develop close relationships. Group living offers protection. It also means following rules and resolving disagreements to keep the group together.

JUST US ▲

Gibbons like to keep their group small. The typical gibbon family has a mother, father, and as many as four offspring. The parents are very protective of their territory and will argue or even fight with other families over the boundaries.

MAKING UP

When a fight breaks out between members of a chimpanzee group, the dispute gets resolved. Chimps often make up within a half-hour. One chimp will approach the other with an outstretched arm or open hand.

Black-and-white colobus monkeys usually travel in small groups—one male with several females and their babies.

▼ REGROUPING

Spider monkeys form groups of about 20 members, but also break into smaller groups to forage for food.

CLEANING UP

For apes and monkeys, grooming is a great way to get rid of any dirt or insects caught in their hair. But most importantly, grooming establishes and strengthens relationships. Some monkeys spend as much as five hours each day grooming.

SOCIAL LADDER ▶

Macaque society is very well-organized, with every member having a rank. High-ranking members eat first, take the best resting spot, and travel in the center of the group. Each monkey inherits its status from its mother, but, if strong and courageous, may earn a higher position on the social ladder.

These red-faced Japanese macaques live in groups of about 200.

SWINGING BABIES

As mammals, the babies of apes and monkeys survive on their mother's milk. For warmth and protection, they cling to their mother until they are big enough to move about on their own.

AMAZON▶
TWINS
Most monkeys and apes give birth to a single infant. The marmosets of the Amazon are one of the few exceptions. They usually have twins.

HANG TIGHT ▲
Apes and monkeys are always on the move, and there's no time to stop for a struggling infant. Mothers go about their regular business—climbing, hanging, leaping from one limb to another—all with baby on board.

SHOW OF COLOR
Babies need special care. One way to get it is to look really different from the adults—by being bright orange! In contrast to its gray relatives, this colorful silver leaf monkey seems to "scream" for everyone's attention. But in adulthood it, too, will grow gray fur.

18

PLAYTIME

Playing games and goofing off is as much fun for young apes and monkeys as it is for you. During play, youngsters make friendships that can last throughout their life. Playing also helps young monkeys learn the rules of the group.

▼ Wrestling on a limb develops the muscles and reflexes of these two young Japanese macaques.

▲ For a young proboscis monkey, playing with a fat tail is just as much fun as climbing a tree.

ALL GROWN UP ▲

Male mountain gorillas acquire the silver hair on their back around age 10. At this point they must leave the group. They may live alone for a while, but will gradually find female gorillas from other groups to join them and help start their own troop.

TAKING CARE

Many monkey and ape dads protect their family. But caring for babies often falls to the female. Among langurs, females gather around a new baby, as if asking the mother for a chance to hold it. The mother lets them, but if danger approaches, she grabs the baby and dashes up a tree.

19

FUNKY MONKEYS

What does it take to set a monkey apart from the others? Maybe an extraordinary nose or a colorful face? If so, these monkeys take the prize.

LONG LEGS ▼

Reaching speeds of 35 miles per hour, the patas monkey is the fastest around, and long legs are part of its secret. Because it stays mostly on the ground, ranging the plains of Africa with hyenas and leopards, its speed is a much needed defense.

◀ BIG-EYED

The night monkey, with its very large round eyes, is the only monkey in the world that is *nocturnal*, or active at night. Found in Central and South America, night monkeys feed on fruit and leaves, and sleep in hollow trees during the day. Not surprisingly, they are also called owl monkeys.

BATHING BEAUTIES

Monkeys taking a bath? Not exactly. In the cold, snowy mountains of Japan, these macaques sit in hot springs just to get warm.

NOSEY GUY

With his large fleshy nose, the male *proboscis* (meaning nose) monkey got his name fair and square. These monkeys are found only on the island of Borneo, Malaysia, where they live in swamp forests and along creeks near the sea. They are good swimmers, and can even swim underwater.

◀ LIP FLIP

Geladas are large monkeys with a patch of naked, pink skin on their chest. These baboons have a strange-looking way of baring their teeth and gums. They flip back their lip!

◀ BLUSHER

The uakari (wah-CAR-ee), has a red face and bald head! It's an amazingly expressive monkey. When really angry or excited, its face turns even brighter. If it feels threatened, it shakes the branches and makes a noise that sounds like laughter.

COLOR COUNTS ▼

A male mandrill has bright blue cheeks and a red nose, which brightens when he is challenged. If that isn't enough to discourage outsiders, he has very sharp canines, four inches long!

21

INCREDIBLE CHIMPS

Chimps are so inventive, they've been known to make their own "shoes"—using twigs as sandals to protect their feet from thorns! They also use rocks to crack open nuts, eat bitter plants to cure stomachaches, and hunt in organized groups.

ALL SIZED UP

Stand next to a common adult male chimp and you'll find he's not very small. He may reach five feet in height and weigh as much as 170 pounds. A second species, known as bonobos, are almost the same size. They live in the rain forests of Zaire, whereas the common chimp ranges the forests and savannas of western and central Africa.

HANG ON, KID

Getting around means hanging on to mother. Baby chimps cling to their mother as soon as they're born and stay close to her for about five years. Wherever she goes, the baby chimp is aboard for the ride.

WHAT A HOOT

With up to 120 members living in their group, chimps have to communicate. When they find food, they hoot, scream, and slap logs. Even young chimps can make as many as 32 different sounds.

EXPRESS YOURSELF

On seeing a waterfall, one group of chimpanzees performed a dance, as if awed by the water. Chimps say a lot with their body, especially their face. They pout when they surrender to an attacker, and grin when excited or afraid. They can also look thoughtful or disbelieving.

REAL PERSONALITY

Can you tell one chimp from another? Next time you go to the zoo, spend some time with these primates. Their face, voice, walk, and personality are so different from one another that it takes primatologists just a few days to easily distinguish 20 or more chimps.

BIG DIET

At one time, people thought chimps were strictly plant eaters. But primatologist Jane Goodall discovered that chimps on occasion also eat meat, such as monkeys, pigs, birds, and antelopes. They may eat a quarter-pound of meat in one day when hunting.

FIERCE FIGHTS

We usually think of chimpanzees as fun-loving and silly. But fights between male chimps over leadership can result in serious injuries. In one population, neighboring bands of chimpanzees were even observed waging deadly war.

This young chimp has only fun in mind! ▶

23

ORANGUTANS

Found only in portions of Borneo and Sumatra, this reddish-brown ape is known as the orangutan, or "person of the forest." The name suits it because an orangutan hardly ever comes out of the trees, living as much as 100 feet above the forest floor.

FRUIT LOVERS

The orangutan, who spends more than half the day eating, is the largest fruit-eating animal in the world. In the tropical forests, different kinds of fruit become ripe at different times of the year. The orangutan eats figs, mangoes, and its favorite fruit—the large, prickly durian. When fruit can't be found, the orangutan dines on leaves and bark.

NOTABLE LIPS

Orangutan lips come in handy when both hands and feet are needed to travel. Opened wide, they can hold a large piece of fruit. Orangutans also use their lips to feel the fruit, puckering up and touching them to the surface.

SHOUT IT OUT

A male orangutan's territory is about two square miles, and he shouts a clear warning to protect it. His morning "long call" is a series of roars and groans that can go on for nearly five minutes. Even in the dense growth of the rain forest, the call is heard by other orangutans as far as a mile away.

WILD LOOKS

Orangutans have some pretty wild looks—with arms one-and-a-half times longer than their legs. And they are not so small. The males are about five feet tall and 220 pounds. The females are about half as heavy.

◀ With age, the male orangutan develops large cheek and chest pouches which frame his face.

ESCAPE ARTIST

There is no doubt that orangutans are smart. In zoos, they're known as escape artists. An orangutan named Bob broke out of three different cages at the San Diego Zoo, including one that had successfully held lions and grizzly bears.

LONERS

The orangutan is the most unsociable of all apes and monkeys. Male orangutans are loners. After mating with a female, they return to their solitary life. Mothers will sometimes feed and travel with other females and their young, but only for a short time. Baby orangutans stay with their mom for about six years.

ACROBATIC

Orangutans are great acrobats. Their strong arms, which span eight feet, really get them around. They prefer to travel by swinging rather than by walking on the ground. In fact, down on the ground orangutans are quite clumsy.

25

THE GREATEST APE

When early European explorers came back from Africa, they told fantastic stories about the gorilla's enormous size and savage temper. African gorillas are huge, but they are also very shy and peaceful. Their only natural enemies are people.

LAID BACK

Gorillas take it easy. They only travel about 400 yards per day. The gorillas get up at dawn to begin feeding; then they move into their nest of leaves and grasses for the afternoon, where adults relax and groom, and youngsters play. In late afternoon they rise to feed again, but by sunset they're back in their nest for the night.

SHOW OFF ▼

When two gorilla groups meet, things can be tense. The dominant male silverbacks may put on elaborate, lengthy displays to intimidate one another—glaring, hooting, chest-beating, and standing on two legs. Each leader is concerned about protecting his troop.

THE BOSS

It's an awesome sight when a male silverback stands upright and begins hooting and chest-beating. His actions mean different things depending on the situation. He may be warning his group of danger or telling a male intruder he is not welcome.

26

◄ A COOL DRINK

Gorillas feed heavily on succulent (water-holding) plants, such as wild celery. Since these plants are so rich in water, gorillas seldom have need for drinking water in the wild. A thirsty gorilla can also usually find a leaf with rain or condensation on it, and lick off the water.

SMART TALKER ▼

Apes are great communicators. One famous gorilla named Koko, who lives at the Gorilla Foundation, has even learned to use more than 500 words in American Sign Language. For her twenty-fifth birthday, Koko asked for a box of "scary" rubber snakes and lizards!

▲ A female's closest relationships are with the silverback and her babies.

NOSEPRINTS

Like human fingerprints, each gorilla has a unique noseprint—the lines above the nostrils. The flare or shape of a gorilla's nostrils are also unique. Researchers use these visual marks to identify each gorilla in a group.

27

TO THE RESCUE

Apes and monkeys are quickly disappearing as forests and grasslands are cleared for farms, houses, and roads. More than 50 percent of these and other primates are considered endangered at this time. But many people are working very hard to save them.

ZOO DUTY ▲

Through breeding and reintroduction programs, zoos are helping endangered apes and monkeys. Young golden lion tamarins born in zoos are taught how to find food and live in the wild. Eventually they are released back into their South American home.

▼ The endangered cotton-top tamarin is being bred in zoos.

In the eyes of a caged chimp, there is only sadness.

AWAY WITH CAGES

Zoos have made a tremendous effort to create living conditions very similar to an animal's natural habitat. So if you visit a zoo, you probably will not see apes and monkeys in cages. They have trees to climb, vines on which to swing, and grassy areas where they can play.

APE HERO

Might the peaceful, intelligent gorilla have compassion for human life? Think of the gorilla, Binti. In 1996, she rescued a three-year-old boy who fell 18 feet into the gorilla exhibit at Brookfield Zoo in Illinois. She picked the boy up, cradled him, then carried him to the zookeepers' door.

Some monkeys can adapt to major changes in their habitat. In Costa Rica, after its forest habitat was cleared for farming, the white-faced capuchin monkey learned to travel on fences instead of trees, and switched to eating food found in cattle pastures and fruit plantations.

GOOD GOODALL ▶

For decades, Jane Goodall studied chimps in the wild. But her work did not stop when she left the field. She set up sanctuaries for orphaned chimps, persuaded scientists to improve conditions for the chimps used in medical research, and began speaking to people about habitat loss in Africa.

LIFE'S WORK

Mountain gorillas received life-saving assistance from researcher Dian Fossey, who lived among these apes from 1963 to 1985. Besides gathering remarkable information, she saved them from extinction by chasing off poachers and making the world aware of gorilla endangerment.

At the edge of the shrinking forest, these gorillas investigate a farmer's expanding field.

29

GLOSSARY

Brachiate: To move by using the arms to swing from one hold, such as a tree branch, to another. Monkeys and apes brachiate as they move through the trees.

Canine teeth: Sharp, pointed teeth. Most meat-eating mammals have four canine teeth in the front of their jaws.

Cheek pouch: A large pocket inside the cheek on both sides of the face. Baboons, macaques, and other monkeys store food in these pouches.

Chest-beating: Beating the chest with the hands. Male gorillas often chest-beat as a way of communicating with other males.

Communicate: To exchange information. Apes and monkeys communicate through sound and movement.

Crustaceans: Class of animals with jointed legs and a hard outer covering; includes lobsters and crabs.

Display: Attention-getting behavior by male animals for the purpose of attracting females during the mating season.

Dominant male: The most important male in a flock, clan, or gathering of animals. The dominant male monkey or ape makes decisions for the rest of his troop.

Endangered: Threatened with extinction. Certain species of apes and monkeys are in danger of becoming extinct (dying out).

Habitat: The place where an animal or plant naturally lives and grows.

Ischial callosite: A hairless pad of skin on each side of the tail of Old World monkeys. These pads enable the monkeys to sleep comfortably while sitting up.

Knuckle-walk: Walking on two feet while bearing the weight of the upper body on the front of the hands, or knuckles. Apes knuckle-walk, but monkeys do not.

Long call: A clear warning shout or roar voiced by a male orangutan to warn predators away from his territory.

Mammals: Warm-blooded animals that nourish their young with milk and have skin covered with hair. Humans and apes are mammals.

New World monkeys: Monkeys that live in South and Central America.

Nocturnal: Active at night. Some primates are nocturnal hunters.

Noseprint: The lines above a gorilla's nostrils. Like human fingerprints, each gorilla has a unique nose print.

Old World monkeys: Monkeys that live in Africa and Southeast Asia.

Opposable thumb: The first finger of the hands of humans, apes, and monkeys. This thumb is opposable to the tips of the other fingers, acting as a clamp for holding objects.

Poacher: A person who hunts animals illegally.

Predator: An animal that hunts other animals for food.

Prey: An animal that is hunted by other animals.

Primate: Member of an order of mammals that includes humans, apes, monkeys, lemurs, and tarsiers.

Primatologist: A person who studies primates.

Proboscis: Nose. The proboscis monkey has a large and unusual-looking nose.

Prosimian: One of the two main groups of the primate order. Lemurs, lorises, and tarsiers are prosimians.

Sanctuary: Any area established for the protection of animals or natural resources.

Status: Position or rank in relation to others. Male apes and monkeys will often fight to establish their status within their troop.

Stereoscopic vision: The ability to see in three dimensions rather than two. Apes and monkeys, like humans, have stereoscopic vision.

Succulents: Plants containing a large quantity of juice or water in their leaves or stems.

Troop: A flock of animals or birds that provide each other with protection. Most apes and monkeys live in troops.